MW00681027

Issues Related
to Parenting

Issues Related to Parenting

By J. Luke Martin

Rod and Staff Publishers, Inc.
P.O. Box 3, Hwy. 172
Crockett, Kentucky 41413
Telephone: (606) 522-4348

Copyright 1995, 2003
by
Rod and Staff Publishers, Inc.
Crockett, Kentucky 41413

Printed in U.S.A

ISBN 978-07399-2328-3

Catalog no. 2601

3   4   5   6   7   —   21   20   19   18   17   16   15   14   13   12

Introduction

Training children in the twenty-first century can be a perplexing undertaking. There are many voices and conflicting ideas and opinions, many of which are simply man's ideas and philosophies. God, the Creator of parents, children, and homes, has given us principles in His Word, the Bible, that are absolutely reliable. Parents of every generation who have laid aside their own ideas and arguments and have, by faith, applied God's tried and proven principles have been richly blessed with happy, well-adjusted, obedient children.

This book holds forth the principles of the Bible and gives practical guidelines for successful parenting. May it make a difference in the lives and eternal destiny of many children.

—Clifford Nolt

Contents

"And they brought young children to him, that he should touch them: and his disciples rebuked those that brought them. But when Jesus saw it, he was much displeased, and said unto them, Suffer the little children to come unto me, and forbid them not: for of such is the kingdom of God. Verily I say unto you, Whosoever shall not receive the kingdom of God as a little child, he shall not enter therein."

Mark 10:13–15

1.

Practical Helps in Relating to Children

Children are not born to seasoned, experienced grandparents, but to inexperienced—and sometimes young and immature—parents. We believe that God has a definite purpose for this. Jesus said, "Without me ye can do nothing"—that is, nothing of any value or spiritual significance. Our success and effectiveness as Christian parents depends primarily on our dependence upon and commitment to Jesus Christ as our teacher, example, and source of wisdom.

The Bible gives us insights into godly homes such as Abraham and Sarah's, Amram and Jochebed's, Elkanah and Hannah's, and Lois and Eunice's. It also exposes the failure and weaknesses of homes like Eli's, David's, and Solomon's. We can learn something from all of them.

The Bible does not provide an outlined, detailed, step-by-step procedure to follow in training a child from day one to the age of twenty-one. It does give various principles that, if faithfully followed, will establish credibility and ensure God's blessing.

Diligence, faith, conviction, wisdom, and courage are some of the qualities that parents need. However, genuine love is the most important. Without it our best efforts will be in vain. Love must be the motivation of all that we do. Children need to be received and appreciated as gifts from God. Parents' greatest interest should be the physical, emotional, and spiritual well-being of their children. Parents who truly love their children will consider no sacrifice too great to meet the needs of their children.

The New Testament assumes that godly parents will endeavor to raise and nurture their children in a godly way. "And, ye fathers, provoke not your children to wrath: but bring them up in the nurture and admonition of the Lord" (Ephesians 6:4). One qualification for a church leader is that he rule well his own house, having his children in subjection with all gravity. See 1 Timothy 3:4, 12 and Titus 1:6.

Bringing up children in the nurture and admonition of the Lord is not an option for Christian parents. It is a command to be taken seriously. As parents, we should never pursue raising children with a "hit or miss" mentality. Rather, we accept the fact that nurturing children is a God-given responsibility involving eternal consequences. If we fail, we will suffer loss. Our failure could well be the cause of a soul being lost forever in a destiny of torment.

As already mentioned, there are no cut-and-dried methods that guarantee absolute success. However, the wise parent knows that God has promised divine guidance, wisdom, and grace to those who seek His face and follow His directions.

"And all thy children shall be taught of the LORD; and great shall be the peace of thy children" (Isaiah 54:13). Our children are to be taught of the Lord as we parents earnestly follow the Lord Jesus and perpetuate in their hearts and minds the principles He taught.

The fact that every child is different and that each has his own personality adds greatly to the challenge of being a successful parent. Some children are mild, easygoing, responsive, and easily disciplined. Others are pronouncedly self-willed, aggressive, and stubborn. I remember one occasion when our fourteen-month-old child defied every effort on my part to restrain and discipline. In helplessness

14

and desperation, I cried to God and asked Him if this was the way I was responding to His love and discipline in my life.

Our children's behavior patterns may well be a mirror, reflecting how we are responding to our heavenly Father. Lack of humility, obedience, and commitment on the part of either parent will be magnified in our children's behavior.

We cannot train children into the kingdom of God. Therefore, we confess that children who come to spiritual birth (are born anew by the Holy Spirit) are saved by the grace of God as they choose to believe in the redemptive work of Christ. At the same time, we also confess that as parents we are largely responsible for our children's acceptance or rejection of the Gospel of Jesus Christ.

Let us take up the challenge of parenting with this perspective.

15

"And these words, which I command thee this day, shall be in thine heart: and thou shalt teach them diligently unto thy children, and shalt talk of them when thou sittest in thine house, and when thou walkest by the way, and when thou liest down, and when thou risest up."

Deuteronomy 6:6, 7

2.

Preparation for Training

The apostle Paul admonishes, in 1 Timothy 5:14, that "the younger women marry, bear children, guide the house, give none occasion to the adversary to speak reproachfully." Such a responsibility calls for much consideration.

Theodore Roosevelt once said, "The task of motherhood and fatherhood, the task of providing for the home and keeping it, is the

17

greatest fundamental task of humanity. If Mother does not do her duty, there will either be no next generation or a generation that is *worse* than none at all."

Hezekiah recognized the divine responsibility placed upon every father when he wrote: "The father to the children shall make known thy truth" (Isaiah 38:19). Paul exhorted the fathers of the church at Ephesus: "Ye fathers, provoke not your children to wrath: but bring them up in the nurture and admonition of the Lord" (Ephesians 6:4). We must not underestimate the influence of a godly mother, but the greater responsibility rests upon the father. God held Eli accountable for his sons' vile behavior and his neglect in correcting them. God also blessed Abraham for faithfully commanding his children and household after him.

1. Prospective parents need to seek the face of God as Manoah and his wife did. "Then Manoah intreated the LORD, and said, O my LORD, let the man of God which thou didst send come again unto us, and teach us what we shall do unto the child that shall be born" (Judges 13:8).

The answer to that prayer is significant. Except for the fact that Samson was to be a Nazarite, the instruction was directly pointed toward the behavior of the mother. She was to be a living example of what God was asking of her son. She was not to eat anything that grew on the vine, drink wine or strong drink, or eat any unclean thing (verse 14). The angel was saying that explicit obedience and commitment on the mother's part was a prime essential for Samson's success.

Parents who sincerely desire guidance in training their children will open their hearts wide to spiritual instruction. They will not only search the Scriptures, but also listen to others with experience. Such parents will be observant. Why are some homes vibrant with harmony, good-will, and success, while others seem to be failures? Although numerous factors may contribute to the answer to this question, one thing is certain: "Except the LORD build the house, they labour in vain that build it" (Psalm 127:1). The Lord will build our home to the degree that we as weak, mortal parents rely on His grace and wisdom.

2. Prospective parents need to consider that giving birth to children is much more than a physical accomplishment. Spiritual powers are at work and eternal destinies are involved.

A father was once congratulated on the birth of his fifth child, second son. His response was, "Oh, it's just another mouth to feed." That son has grown to manhood and is taking a fling in the world. His siblings appear to be faithful to the Lord. Possibly the father's implication that this son was just a physical existence conveyed more than the father realized. It is true that providing physical substance—food, clothing, medicine, and so forth—requires much time, effort, and money. Yet that is not the real purpose of our life or being. The real issues of life are spiritual.

20

They are deeply rooted in our concept of the nature of God and in the conscious choices we make in the way we serve Him.

Children soon learn this fact. They will never be fooled as to what holds priority in the home. Positive, indelible impressions are made when children see their parents sacrifice the physical and material in preference of spiritual values.

3. Husband and wife need to communicate with each other concerning the specific details and values that are important in the nurture of children. Then they need to decide how they can best implement these convictions.

This kind of communication takes time. It requires up-front honesty. Do we sense God's approval? Is God satisfied with our efforts? Are the children responding favorably and willingly? Are we conveying mutual interest in each child's personal development? Are we overlooking any carnal traits in our children's behavior?

Fathers and mothers may have different

perspectives on how to relate to specific needs. Mother feels that Father is intimidating in his method of addressing the needs in the children. Father thinks that Mother is too sharp with her tongue and speaks too harshly. Many parents react to each other's particular way of relating to the children. Instead of helping each other improve through honest and humble communication, they insist on their own way and complicate the situation.

In contrast, parents who learn to share together their observations of each other's weaknesses and encourage each other will soon experience harmony and progress. Only then can we effectively pray for God's blessing in the training and nurturing of our children.

4. Parents who react carnally to their children's misbehavior plant seeds of confusion in the children's mind and frustrate their emotional development. Why would parents who profess to be followers of the meek and lowly

Jesus display contempt, ridicule, anger, scorn, or rejection? It is right and proper to express disapproval, disappointment, and concern. This, however, needs to be expressed in love, fairness, and understanding. Godly love does not overlook failure or wrong conduct. It disciplines to correct the wrongdoing and establishes patterns of acceptable behavior. The parents' personal examples of spiritual transformation by the grace of God is of critical importance.

5. Prospective parents who are serious about raising obedient children will identify and submit to other spiritually-minded believers in the church. This sets a precedent for requiring obedience and submission from their children. Children are blessed indeed when they see their parents faithfully serving the Lord Jesus together with other believers. Parents who refuse to submit to the spiritual authority over them (Hebrews 13:7, 17) greatly hinder their effectiveness in raising godly children.

23

Issues Related to Parenting

There is no such thing as perfect parents. With the best of intentions and commitment, areas of weakness and blindness will exist. The combined strengths of a variety of homes blended together in Scriptural church life provide the greatest potential for success.*

---

* A Scriptural congregation is one that operates according to the Biblical principles of discipleship and cross bearing. Such a congregation will give guidance to its members to help them in the daily issues of life such as child training.

"The L<small>ORD</small> is nigh unto all them that call upon him, to all that call upon him in truth. He will fulfil the desire of them that fear him: he also will hear their cry, and will save them."

Psalm 145:18, 19

3.

The Value and Potential of the Child

All adults began as innocent infants. Only as infants grow to maturity and begin to make choices are destinies determined. Just think of influential men of the recent past. Adolf Hitler and Daniel Kauffman both started life as innocent babies, but, oh, what contrasts they were by the end of their lives! What part did training or the lack of it contribute to their destinies?

The Struggle Between God and Satan for the Child

We believe that next to God, Satan knows best the potential of a godly seed. The scene in Revelation 12 pictures Satan ready to devour the Christ-child at His birth. Certainly Almighty God's intervention should provide young parents with a tremendous anchor of faith that the same deliverance is available for their own children.

But bear in mind that just as Satan sought to destroy the Christ-child from birth, he will seek to destroy the seed of every godly parent, not necessarily physically, but rather spiritually through a subtle, scheme of "innocent" tolerance, negligence, and compromise on the part of the parents themselves.

Consider some Bible examples. God promised Abraham that through his seed all the families of the earth would be blest. This was a prophetic message concerning Jesus Christ. Working through Pharaoh, Satan decreed that every male Hebrew infant be cast into

28

the Nile River. But praise God, one home refused to cooperate with Satan's plan.

Later God promised David that of his seed there would arise a King who would reign forever. Again we see Satan working through wicked Athaliah, who determined to destroy all the *seed* royal. Again his plan was thwarted. Faithful Jehosheba rescued Joash and hid him.

Lastly, we see Satan making one last effort through King Herod to destroy the Christ-child of Bethlehem. Yet He who was the promised seed of the woman was divinely preserved. Just so, there is also hope for every child whose parents seek the face of God and follow His command.

Spiritual Lessons of Childhood

Someone once asked the question, "Why was it necessary for Jesus to come as a babe?" The answer came back: "Because that is the only way we can come to Him." So it is. Jesus said that except we become as *little* children, we cannot enter the kingdom of heaven. While the human mind cannot comprehend the full purposes of God in the Incarnation, certainly this aspect is one vital truth concerning it.

In Isaiah's time of gloom and doom, the hope of Israel did not lie in a full-grown man, but in a child (Isaiah 7:14). In 9:6 the child again appears as the one who will be the ultimate ruler, not only of Israel but of all the redeemed. Again, in 11:6, it is the child who is the pictured emblem of Christ's kingdom of peace. In the child all God's purposes lie latent. As children come to maturity, God's purposes begin to be realized, provided the child has been given the proper training and of his own volition makes right choices.

Paul admonished the Corinthians, "In malice be ye children, but in understanding be men" (1 Corinthians 14:20). Children forgive and forget their childish disagreements very easily. As adults, we should learn a lesson from them. With the understanding of men we should choose the way of forgiveness and learn its eternal value.

Children's Prayer

In the early morning, when the sunbeams bright
    Shine around our pathway, scattering the night,
Jesus, gentle Saviour, hear our earnest prayer:
    Bless the little children; take us in Thy care.

When temptations gather, fears or foes affright,
    When our footsteps waver in the path of right,
Jesus, tender Saviour, with Thine arm uphold;
    All our upward strivings in Thy love enfold.

When the shadows lengthen, bringing sweet repose,
    Weary hands are folded, little eyelids close,
Jesus, loving Saviour, guard us through the night;
    Keep Thy little children safe till morning light.

"And the child grew, and waxed strong in spirit, filled with wisdom: and the grace of God was upon him. . . . And he said unto them, How is it that ye sought me? wist ye not that I must be about my Father's business?"

Luke 2:40, 49

4.

The Child—a Threefold Being

The Bible speaks of man as a threefold being—spirit, soul, and body. Infants are that at birth, yet parents tend naturally to concentrate primarily on the nurture of the body. The infant is fed, clothed, and sheltered with the best of care.

1. The Child's Spirit

In Genesis 2:7 we read, "The LORD God formed man . . . and breathed into his nostrils the breath of life; and man became a living soul." The spirit of the child is the very life of the child. It is also that inner consciousness by which the child comes to know himself as a person. It is within the child's spirit that he develops a consciousness of God and all other personalities.

Through his spirit the child senses acceptance or rejection, tension or rest, love or animosity, happiness or sadness. The child is sensitive to these emotions very early, long before he or she can talk or communicate.

Ministering to a child's spirit should become a primary goal of every sincere parent and should begin even before birth. Women who are frustrated and resentful of their calling are already sending a negative signal to the unborn. Parents who argue and quarrel or speak harshly are also conveying a message. In contrast, parents who trust, pray, sing, and communicate with each other in love provide an atmosphere

34

of rest that gives the unborn a tremendous advantage.

Perhaps a hospital experiment will help us to more readily comprehend these facts. A certain hospital that specializes in prenatal care played soft music and hymns to a control group of premature babies. A second group heard no music. The first group gained considerably faster. There was also a third group for which they played rock music. The hospital soon had to abandon this experiment because these infants began to lose weight and became very colicky.

Infants whose mothers cuddle them and who call them often by their own name have been proven to respond to other stimuli at a more rapid rate than infants who do not receive such attentions. Coupling this with reading Bible stories and singing children's lullabies over and over again brings an unspoken comfort and security to the infant's spirit, even before he or she can articulate words.

2. The Child's Soul

The terms *spirit* and *soul* are sometimes used interchangeably in the Bible and refer to the same thing. Yet in definition we distinguish the soul as the very character of the individual as expressed in the intellect, the emotions, and the will.

Parents look forward with keen anticipation to the development of their newborn infant's understanding. That first smile, the particular noticing of bright objects, the first semblance of syllables that sound like *Mama* or *Papa* are met with great delight. Parents who give studied attention to help a young child develop his intellect at a very young age contribute both to his capacity to learn and to his ability to grasp facts when he enters school. This requires intentional communication.

Showing him an object such as a ball or a baby in a book and then asking him to identify it helps the young child begin to make rational decisions. Reading the same story over and over, particularly a Bible story with pictures, and then asking questions about the various illustrations in the picture stimulates the child's mind. This routine should begin before the child can talk. It teaches him to think.

A child expresses his feelings through emotion. The wise parent will pay attention to the child's cry or laughter. An infant usually cries when he is hungry or in pain. It may be he has some other discomfort or senses fear. Discerning the reason for an infant's continued crying is not always easy. Sometimes the cry reflects the tensions of a tired nursing mother.

As the infant grows a little older, he may cry because of anger over some discomfort. At this juncture the infant may be too small to spank, yet a firm hold and a gentle "no, no" registers a mental impression on his spirit. Consistently following this pattern at an early stage teaches the child that the emotions must also be controlled. It is right to let the child cry for a short time after he is corrected, but continuous crying that ends in pouting calls for more correction.

Closely related to the emotions is the child's will. Every child is born with an Adamic nature that will very early express itself in selfishness. The young child knows only his own interests, not anyone else's hunger, feelings, or desires. The child's will demands that his needs and desires be satisfied right now. Although immediate gratification may be necessary at the start, it is good to bring the child into a routine schedule in order to teach him that his will needs to be subject to order and discipline. The more consistently this is done, the easier it will be for the child to learn the blessing of other boundaries that his parents establish.

A child must be taught very early that he must submit his will to the will of his parents. The parent chooses the play area, decides which toys are allowed, and how the toys must be shared with other siblings if there are any. It is for the parents to decide when candy may be eaten and how much. Invariably the child's will will run counter to these restrictions. Yet it is in these small, seemingly easily overlooked issues that indelible impressions are made on the intellect, emotions, and will of the child.

3. The Child's Body

God created man with a visible, physical body. It is this living physical body that becomes the joy of the new mother and father when the first cry of life issues from the infant's lips.

One of the first efforts of the parent is to clothe the newborn and then to proceed to give nourishment. This was true of Mary, the mother of the Christ-child. "And she brought forth her firstborn son, and wrapped him in swaddling clothes" (Luke 2:7).

This inborn, natural response to clothe and feed the body can become a snare that Satan can and has used to trap many well-meaning parents. Many mothers not only see the necessity of clothing their children, but also yield to the temptation to doll them up. Such a temptation is very subtle. Parents, instead of conscientiously giving precedence to the nurture of the child's spirit and soul, too often concentrate on his physical development and appearance. Jesus' question in Matthew 6:25 strikes to the core of this issue. "Is not the life more than meat, and the body than raiment?"

Why is the outward adorning of the body a continuous issue among Christian people? Does not the answer lie in the fact that many fathers and mothers have succumbed to the temptation of considering it acceptable to lavish their pride and secret love for bodily adornment on their children? Accenting bodily adornment over and above character development establishes in a child's mentality a precedent that becomes deeply rooted. Satan would have it so.

Conscientious parents will see that their children are properly fed and clothed. Yet their paramount concern is the nurture and development of the child's spirit and character. We believe that it was so in Jesus' home. The result was that Jesus grew in wisdom and stature and in favor with God and man.

Children who are taught to keep the body in subjection to spiritual law make a greater and better contribution to the church than those taught otherwise. The ones who become enslaved to bodily adornment smother their usefulness in the kingdom.

"By faith Moses, when he was come to years, refused to be called the son of Pharaoh's daughter; choosing rather to suffer affliction with the people of God, than to enjoy the pleasures of sin for a season; esteeming the reproach of Christ greater riches than the treasures in Egypt: for he had respect unto the recompence of the reward. By faith he forsook Egypt, not fearing the wrath of the king: for he endured, as seeing him who is invisible."

Hebrews 11:24-27

5.

The Child's First Years

The Biblical account in Hebrews 11 of Moses' understanding and the choices he made when he came to maturity is simply amazing. Taken from his parental home at a very young age and thrust into the culture and learning of pagan Egypt, he nevertheless maintained some valuable truth. The martyr Stephen said that Moses was learned in all the wisdom of Egypt and was mighty in words and deeds (Acts 7:22).

According to the account in Hebrews 11:24–27, Moses (1) knew who the people of God really were; (2) understood that while sin may offer some physical pleasure, it only lasts for a season; (3) knew and believed about the coming Messiah; (4) correctly evaluated that heavenly rewards are of greater value than earthly treasure; (5) knew that the invisible God could protect him from the anger of a powerful earthly king; and (6) possessed the character to do what was right, regardless of what it cost him.

He did all this by faith. Romans 10:17 says that "faith cometh by hearing." Where did Moses hear? He certainly did not acquire faith from a Bible in Pharaoh's library! No, he heard these valuable eternal truths from the lips of his mother and father. He must have heard them over and over at a very young age. His parents had a vision.

We do not believe that children are capable of experiencing Scriptural conversion (the

44

new birth) at a very young age, as child evangelists promote, but we do believe in Biblical nurturing. It is important and right that we fill the child's mind with all the *facts* of truth that the child is capable of absorbing.

A teacher of first grade students had the policy of quizzing beginners on their knowledge of simple Bible stories. Such a survey was often disheartening. Many pupils were ignorant of who the first people were who lived on the earth. Some seemingly had never heard about Noah and the Flood, Joseph, or Daniel. This is a serious indictment against the parents of these children.

Parents often take too much for granted. They assume that little children will just catch on. But the Bible commands that they be taught. We live in a fast-moving society, but nothing should ever replace the bedtime Bible story, prayer, and the routine schedule of teaching small children the moral law of right behavior.

The one supreme fact that should be

indelibly impressed on the small child's mind is that of God. It is God who gives us food and clothes. It is God who created the beautiful world and makes the sun to shine and sends the rain. It is God who heals injuries and makes sick people well. It is God we adore and worship when we gather for the public meeting. It is to God they say their bedtime prayers before climbing into bed.

This is not trying to make "little Christians" out of our children. It is simply establishing within them a consciousness that Father and Mother love God and that God loves them all. It also establishes a consciousness that everything and every person has meaning because God is the supreme Creator. Certainly children are not able to define these truths, but the facts must be taught in order to provide them with a proper foundation on which to build their developing powers of understanding.

In Our Dear Lord's Garden

In our dear Lord's garden,
    Planted here below,
Many tiny flowers
    In sweet beauty grow.

Jesus loves the children,
    Children such as we;
Blest them when their mothers
    Brought them to His knee.

Lord, Thy call we answer;
    Take us in Thy care;
Train us in Thy garden
    In Thy works to share.

Nothing is too little
    For His gentle care;
Nothing is too lowly
    In His love to share.

"As ye know how we exhorted and comforted and charged every one of you, as a father doth his children."

1 Thessalonians 2:11

6.

Winning the Heart of Your Child

King Solomon, in his God-given wisdom, made many personal appeals to his son. "My son, hear the instruction of thy father, and forsake not the law of thy mother" (Proverbs 1:8). "My son, if sinners entice thee, consent thou not" (1:10). "My son, walk not thou in the way with them" (1:15). "My son, if thou wilt receive my words . . ." (2:1). "My son, forget not my law" (3:1). "My son, despise not the chastening of the LORD" (3:11). "My son, let not them depart from thy eyes" (3:21). "Hear, O my son" (4:10). "My son, attend to my words" (4:20). "My son, attend unto my wisdom" (5:1). "My son, if thou be surety for thy friend . . ." (6:1). "My son, keep thy father's commandment" (6:20). "My son, keep my words" (7:1).

Finally, in Proverbs 23:26, he says, "My son, *give me thine heart,* and let thine eyes observe my ways." It is the heart cry of every Christian parent. We can give the best of instruction. We may have a "perfect" set of rules. We may even command strict obedience. Yet if we do not have our child's heart, we will be disappointed in the fruit of our labors.

What does it mean to have your child's heart? To answer that question honestly, ask yourself as a parent, or teacher, or guardian, who has your heart? Where is your trust, your confidence, your affection? How is your heart won over or moved to yield allegiance to another? God is asking for your heart as a parent. Have you given it to Him?

God has our heart only when we obey Him. Our obedience is to be the voluntary response of love. Only then will God truly have our heart. Likewise, having your child's heart is knowing that it is his desire to please you.

How do we go about achieving a heart-to-heart relationship with our child? There are several factors to be reckoned with in answering this question.

1. Children are born with a selfish nature. Left to themselves, all that children can think about is "what pleases me." In early infancy, we cater to their demands because their demands usually reveal a need or physical discomfort. We keep them warm, and dry, and comfortable. As soon as possible, we interest them in moving objects, picture books, and other items that attract their attention.

It is not long, however, till the child decides he is not happy with his toys or his

51

environment even if his needs are met. Parents should continue to meet the child's needs but not cater to the child's selfish demands. This is the crucial moment in the parent–child relationship. It is at this juncture that modern psychology and the traditional Bible method part ways.

Psychology says, "Give the child what he wants. Don't inhibit any of his expressions or demands. To do so will crush the child's spirit or warp his personality." Is that philosophy working? The answer is no! It has produced a generation with many delinquents, broken homes, and emotionally unstable people.

The Bible way, in contrast, is the discipline of love. "I will therefore that the younger women marry, bear children, guide the house" (1 Timothy 5:14). "One that ruleth well his own house, having his children in subjection with all gravity." (1 Timothy 3:4). "He that spareth his rod hateth his son: but he that loveth him chasteneth him betimes" (Proverbs 13:24).

The child will not be very old until he will need to be restrained. When a child begins to manifest rebellion by making his body stiff or crying after his needs are met, he needs some form of discipline. The four-month-old needs to be held firmly and tightly to feel the strength and security of his parent's arms. The six-month-old may need a spanking.[1] The purpose is to establish a communication of loving restraint through law.

In this early stage, the mother or the father should speak to the child during the discipline process, saying, "No, no," while bringing the child to a place of submission. The child needs to learn early to surrender his will to the will of his parents.

Consistency in the way we discipline is always important. But it is very important in the beginning years. A rule made is a rule

---

[1] Note that ages will vary according to a child's personality. Parents must evaluate each child's needs separately, rather than following an exact formula.

to be obeyed.[2] Any deviation from this principle will confuse the child. It is in this area that many parents fail. Some days we tend to be strict, other days more lenient. If the child pleads and begs and we bend after having said no, we lose.

It is in these early stages that parents must discipline *themselves*. It is not only the fact of what they want their children to *do*, but what they want them to *be*. This requires looking far beyond the present into the future. What do we want our children to become in terms of respect, reverence, decency, and dependability? Keeping the end product in view will help us establish a more consistent pattern of discipline.

Consistency requires that we are there for our child. Being there means that we are always ready to supply sustaining support. A discipline of love not only corrects wrong

---

[2] Evaluate your rules carefully, however, to make sure they are workable. It is better to admit to a child that you made a mistake than to insist on enforcing a foolish rule.

actions, but also gives encouragement for right ones. It pays attention to any difficulty or struggle and lends not only words of encouragement, but also tender guidance, by showing that you understand. When your child knows that you feel with him, you are on the way to winning his heart.

2. Children are born with a sinful nature. God stated that the imaginations of man's heart are evil from his youth (see Genesis 6:5; 8:21). The Bible also says that "foolishness is bound in the heart of a child; but the rod of correction shall drive it far from him" (Proverbs 22:15).

The self-centered nature of the child also expresses itself in lying, quarreling, foolishness, and other aggressive behavior patterns. As these negative patterns begin to emerge, the discipline of law must become more pronounced. The restrictions and force of law will never convert the heart, but they are God's method to bring the will of the child under control. When the pain of chastisement

55

exceeds the gratification of getting his own way, a child can be trained to give up his will in favor of his parents' will. The next chapter will discuss discipline more extensively.

3. Children are born with a teachable nature. All children have a carnal nature from birth. Yet in many ways they come to us as a clean sheet of paper. The habits and character traits that are printed on that paper are the responsibility of the parents.

We often think of teaching as informing and developing the child's intellect. The groundwork, though, must first be laid in teaching the child sound emotional responses. Intellectual understanding without proper emotional control can be counterproductive.

Sound emotional control begins with the communication of love. Why are older women to teach the young mothers to love their children (Titus 2:4)? Does a mother not naturally love her children? Yes, there is a measure of natural love in most parents. This natural love, though, can rise or fall with our feelings. If we feel well and chipper, and the children are behaving agreeably, then we love them. If we feel discouraged, then natural love may give way to harsh, censorious demands.

In contrast, true (or spiritual) love is sacrificial and constant. The child senses and feels loved at all times. He feels accepted and appreciated. True love communicates security and rest. Before parents can communicate this stability of love, they themselves must be rooted in a love relationship with Jesus Christ. The spiritual dimension of such a relationship helps us relate to the child's developing temperament with understanding and patient control.

Teaching a child emotional control is helping the child to control his feelings. A child expresses his feelings through crying, laughing, anger, speaking, and showing affection to others. Without proper guidance and restraint, a child will let his emotions dictate how he responds to any given situation. If he does not get his own way, he will respond in uncontrolled anger, throwing toys, lying on the floor and kicking, or simply screaming. Or if he is in a good mood, he may laugh hilariously. If hurt or sad, he may cry uncontrollably. Some children are inclined to smother their friends with hugs and kisses.

Parental love will not overlook these imbalances, but will carefully help the child bring his feelings under control. How can we do this?

Emotions are the outward expression of a person's feelings. They are the reaction of the body senses—seeing, hearing, feeling, smelling, and tasting. The child who sees and hears Father and Mother quarreling will express fear, distrust, and insecurity. He will also respond in anger when he does not get his own way. The parents in this situation will have a difficult time helping the child to respond appropriately.

Emotions are also the expression of how a person thinks. Expressions of happiness, contentment, goodwill, and thankfulness come from a heart and mind that has been taught by God (1 Thessalonians 4:9). Expressions of self-will, hatred, envy, jealousy, and bitterness come from a heart that has not been sanctified and regenerated by the Spirit of Christ.

We have already mentioned the importance of parents living in a love relationship with Jesus Christ. Such a relationship will be expressed in humility and submission to the will of God. It will respond in constant love, patience, and goodwill toward friends and neighbors. Forgiveness will be shown to those who trespass. Such parents act responsibly because they think right. Sometimes parents may not feel well. They may have been insulted, misunderstood, or intimidated. Or maybe things have gone backward. Maybe two different viewpoints have emerged on a given issue. Godly parents in these situations do not respond according to their feelings, but according to truth. It is a Christ like example of emotional stability to the children.

The first step in teaching emotional control is helping the child to think rightly. He needs to think objectively about his parents, his siblings, his toys, his friends, and his environment. His first impulse by nature is to respond selfishly, and so when parents say no, there will be a natural reaction of feeling that expresses hurt. When this expression is not properly instructed and disciplined with truth and love, the hurt will turn to anger and violence, like hitting back at the parents.

Children can be helped to think right by example and constant communication of facts. For instance, little Johnny is told to share his toy tractor with his brother. He says, "No," and runs the other way. Father tells Johnny to come. He refuses. Father spanks Johnny and tells him to share his tractor. Johnny reluctantly gives up his tractor, but stalks off, pouting. Father spanks Johnny again and tells him how much better it is to share. He shows the boys how to play together and increase each other's happiness.

Or, take Susan for another example. It is 6:30 and the alarm clock is ringing. To Susan, that means getting up and starting the washing machine. But Susan does not feel like getting up. She stays in bed. After the third call, Mother needs to punish Susan for her negligence. Susan reacts and sulks. She begins the wash, but grumbles in the process. Mother has a firm talk with Susan and shows her that obedience and schedules are a vital part of an orderly life. A routine makes work not only bearable, but also enjoyable. As parents teach these basic principles, children learn to think objectively.

Secondly, children need help and direction in reacting to pain, disappointment, and success. It is the natural reaction for children to wail uncontrollably when hurt. While crying can relieve pain to a point, uncontrolled screaming will only increase it. It is important to help your child to control his crying so that he can begin to think rationally. Remember, the child screams to draw attention to himself. By not allowing that kind of emotional response, you can focus the child's attention more toward the fact of what caused the pain and what needs to be done for relief.

Children naturally respond to disappointment by demonstrating anger. John asks for permission to go and play with his neighbor friend, but Father says, "No." When John becomes sulky or angry, Father needs to stop him and explain why such a response is unacceptable. Father takes the time to teach John that life is made up of many disappointments and that sulking or getting angry only adds to the hurt. Accepting a no cheerfully is a step toward positive emotional control.

It is natural for children to boast about their accomplishments. While it is right to feel satisfied when doing our best, bragging and gloating are emotional expressions that warp a child's personality and damage him socially. The wise parent is aware of the destructiveness of pride (Proverbs 16:18) and will encourage and insist on expressions of humility. We do this by teaching our children that the abilities they have are God-given and are to be used for His glory.

Helping children to think and act responsibly requires constant commitment and communication from parents. We cannot afford to leave anything to chance. It is in the daily routine of interacting and paying attention to small details that parents establish a bond of love with their children that communicates acceptance and security. When your children feel secure in your love and commitment, you know you have their heart.

"For whom the Lord loveth he chasteneth, and scourgeth every son whom he receiveth. If ye endure chastening, God dealeth with you as with sons; for what son is he whom the father chasteneth not? . . . Now no chastening for the present seemeth to be joyous, but grievous: nevertheless afterward it yieldeth the peaceable fruit of righteousness unto them which are exercised thereby."

Hebrews 12:6, 7, 11

7.

The Discipline of the Child

"How shall we order the child, and how shall we do unto him?" This was Manoah's question to the angel in regard to their parental responsibility. It will be the honest question of every godly parent. The angel's answer is rather startling. Rather than giving a detailed prescription, he in essence said, "You be disciplined parents." Effective discipline begins with a godly example and authority.

Issues Related to Parenting

Parents are responsible to order the child. Many parents are intimidated and lax because of the pressure from Satan's kingdom to surrender this God-given responsibility. They become fearful of being too strict or too insistent on absolute obedience. We must remember that Satan operates on fear. God's way is the way of faith. He says, "Trust Me."

The Scriptures are emphatic on the divine requirement. "And these words, which I command thee this day, shall be in thine heart: and thou shalt teach them diligently unto thy children, and shalt talk of them when thou sittest in thine house, and when thou walkest by the way, and when thou liest down, and when thou risest up" (Deuteronomy 6:6, 7).

No room is given for laxness, apathy, or excuses. It is a "thou shalt" from God. We are to do it diligently. We are to pursue the responsibility with earnest effort and energy. We need to reach out for input from others. We should be conscious of the effectiveness or ineffectiveness of our methods. We must not be too proud to ask with Manoah, "How shall we order the child, and how shall we do?"

Discipline is often thought of in a negative sense. It is considered some form of punishment or correction for misbehavior. In the *World Book Dictionary* this definition is number 6. The first five definitions have to do with careful training and maintaining order. Remember, Manoah asked, "How shall we *order* the child?" We conclude then that Scriptural discipline is first of all objective measures that establish sound patterns of acceptable conduct. When those patterns of conduct are violated, then action must be taken to correct the violation to restore the established order.

As parents, we tend to extremes in both the objective and corrective aspects of discipline. We can be too "loving" to the point of condoning things we should not or too demanding to the point of discouraging the child. To carry out discipline without being destructive should be a priority of every parent.

When you practice objective discipline,

you open the door of communication between you and your child and keep it open. When you practice objective discipline, you make rules and establish boundaries. When you practice objective discipline, you will be able to explain the Biblical principles for your rules. Such rules should basically center around physical safety and proper social interaction.

Physical safety involves teaching children the danger of fire: Do not play with matches. It requires caution, like looking both ways before crossing a street. It insists on being properly clothed for weather conditions to avoid colds, and so forth. It stresses the foolishness of taking risks such as jumping from excessive heights or doing things just for personal glory. Physical safety does not take chances unless it is an emergency to save someone else.

Making rules for physical safety will go further if there is a corresponding emphasis on the value and sanctity of life. Our bodies belong to God. They are a gift to us from Him. This makes us stewards, not owners.

Then there is the economic factor. Accidents are costly. There is the saying that "an ounce of prevention is worth a pound of cure." Today we could say, "A moment of consideration, caution, and forethought could save thousands of dollars of accident expenses." Add to this the agony and suffering that is caused by breaking safety rules.

Objective social discipline is much more comprehensive yet than physical safety. It is helping children properly adjust to themselves as a person—a soul with a body. It is helping them to relate to other persons with honor and respect.

Children seem to have a natural curiosity about the functions of the physical body. As parents we owe our children the understanding that the body is not sinful. At the same time we help our children understand that many temptations come to them through the body senses and drives.

Objective social discipline teaches respect, reserve, and modesty in relating to the opposite sex. As they grow, brothers and sisters should be taught to keep their hands off each other. Teaching this principle at an early age establishes a precedent that safeguards boys and girls as they mature. See 1 Corinthians 7:1.

Developing proper social interaction is a high priority in parental training and discipline. Young children need supervision, especially when playing or associating with other children. This does not mean they can never be out of our sight. It does mean, however, that we know where they are and what they are doing. It means that our children know they are answerable to us for their talk and behavior.

Showing and expressing interest in our young children's friends is very important. Teaching them how to be good friends is equally important. This will involve teaching them to share their toys, play fairly, lose cheerfully, and express themselves in wholesome language. To do this we must pay close attention to what our children are saying about their friends and activities.

Keeping the door of communication open concerning our children's needs and fears in relating to their peers is so essential. As parents we jealously close the gap between the older and younger generation and express daily interest in how our children are coping with their growing relationships.

Corrective discipline is punishment administered to the child for disobedience. As mentioned before, a rule made is a rule to be obeyed. Breaking the rules should be considered a serious matter that needs immediate attention. Failing to address disobedience paves the way for more criminal behavior. It will also let the child live with the guilt and insecurity.

It is from the Old Testament that we learn the most about corrective punishment for disobedient children. However, the New Testament takes for granted that parents who love their children will chasten them. "For whom the Lord loveth he chasteneth, and scourgeth every son whom he receiveth. If ye endure chastening, God dealeth with you as with sons; for what son is he whom the father chasteneth not? But if ye be without chastisement, whereof all are partakers, then are ye bastards, and not sons. Furthermore we have had fathers of our flesh which *corrected us,* and we gave them reverence: shall we not much rather be in subjection unto the Father of spirits, and live?" (Hebrews 12:6–9).

From this passage we learn that parents who love their children will correct them. We also conclude that parents who neglect to correct their children in essence hate them.

Consider some Old Testament verses.

Proverbs 13:24: "He that spareth his rod hateth his son: but he that loveth him chasteneth him betimes." How can chastening your son with a rod be an expression of love? Using the rod (a slender, somewhat flexible, narrow piece of wood) conveys a message that goes deeper than words. It inflicts pain that is greater than the pleasure the erring child gets from his disobedience. Godly love uses this Bible method to restrain the bent toward self-expression and self-pleasing. It helps the child to focus on what is the better way and the better choice. The rod must be used consistently and applied with enough force to bring the child to a place of submission and repentance for the wrong he has done.

Proverbs 19:18: "Chasten thy son *while there is hope,* and let not thy soul spare for his crying." "While there is hope" implies that we must begin early. At the point that an infant stiffens his back and resists you, he must feel your restraint. As he stiffens himself, hold him firmly, telling him, "No." As he relaxes, slowly relax your hold. This method is one of the earliest forms of correction. A six- to eight-month-old will usually need to be spanked.

This passage also suggests that a child will cry (beyond reason) to excite your sympathy and possibly to express anger for being corrected. Discipline should always be within the limits of self-control and reason. The cry needs to be one of penitence and not rebellion. At times a number of spankings will be required to bring the child to the place of submission.

Proverbs 22:15: "Foolishness is bound in the heart of a child; but the rod of correction shall drive it far from him." This verse corresponds with Genesis 8:21, where God affirms the fact that the imagination of man's heart is evil from his youth. This foolishness in the hearts of our children needs full attention. It is the bent toward self-centeredness and self-expression. It is the absence of wisdom that is gained by instruction, discipline, and experience.

Proverbs 29:15: "The rod and reproof give wisdom: but a child left to himself bringeth his mother to shame."

Proverbs 23:14: "Thou shalt beat him with the rod, and shalt deliver his soul from hell." These verses imply that the proper use of the rod has a direct bearing on the destiny of the child. The rod should never be used as an act of revenge or for the venting of parental anger. It must convey the disapproval of the one administering the discipline. Along with the disapproval must be the reproof of love that explains the reason for the discipline. We simply care too much to let the child develop bad habits or pursue a course that leads to destruction.

The trend in social service interference and the possibility of incrimination for spanking our children is placing an added burden on parenting. We need to be discreet and cautious as to where and how we spank. In fact, knowing what your family doctor would do if he were to find marks on your child is advisable. If he would respond negatively, try to find a doctor who understands your convictions. Avoid spanking in public places. If you are in a church service where visitors are present, be sure to go to a private place if your child needs discipline. If discipline is consistently administered at home, it will greatly reduce the need for spanking in public. Parents who need to do a lot of spanking when away from home should take a closer look at their home training.

In conclusion, remember that, if properly done, most corrective punishment will take place in the first years of a child's life. Most properly corrected children will remember very few spankings. The need for continued spankings as the child gets older may imply that we have failed somewhere to impress upon our child the seriousness of disobedience.

Discipline is most effective when it is consistent. To be strict one day and lenient the next sends the child confusing signals. The child will not only become confused, but frustrated as well. Children perform best when they know what is expected and what will be required.

Along with being consistent, we must avoid nagging, threatening, bribing, begging, and reasoning with our children (especially with younger children). These methods may seem nicer than giving a command and seeing that it is obeyed, but they will only harden the child and destroy the bond of love. These methods do not develop a right concept of authority in the child's mind, neither do they bring the child's will into subjection. A command that is authoritative, without leaving any option except obedience, goes a long way in helping the child develop a right sense of responsibility.

The father is normally the one responsible to establish patterns of discipline in the home. Ephesians 5:23 speaks of the husband as being the "saviour of the body." The father will be held responsible before God for what he has allowed. Father's strong, steady hand is more effective in the discharge of discipline than Mother's tender sympathies. There are exceptions to this fact, we know. There are children who grow up without a father. By the grace of God and the guidance and prayers of a godly mother such children have grown up to be godly men and women.

Mother's role in discipline is unique in its own right. Proverbs 1:8 and 6:20 speak of the law of the mother in conjunction with the father's instruction and commandment.

This law of the mother is the firm conviction of moral responsibility that compels her to duty. It is the exact opposite of the flippant, permissive, indulgent attitudes characteristic of many mothers today. The "law of thy mother" suggests a mother who is paying close attention to small details. It implies that Mother is carefully guarding her child's actions and reactions. These include the way her child plays with his toys and with other children, as well as the child's eating habits. Children need to be taught to eat what is set before them and to be thankful for what they receive.

By keeping their children modestly covered, mothers show their concern about how their children relate to their bodies. They sense responsibility in making and buying consistent clothing. Dresses need to be lengthened as girls grow taller. Fullness needs to be added to the pattern to conceal body features as the body develops.

It is the mother who is most constantly with the child in the early years. She is the one who conveys those early impressions of acceptance and expectations upon the child's consciousness. It is she who will most likely inflict those early punishments that cause the child to submit to her will. Blessed indeed are the children who have a mother who fears God and seeks to guide their feet in right paths.

The father is responsible to support and encourage the mother in fulfilling her role. It is imperative that parents be united in their purpose and methods of discipline, as has already been stated. It is extremely important that fathers and mothers together in private discuss the methods they are employing and evaluate their effectiveness.

Sometimes Father is lax in his duty and needs a gentle reminder from Mother. Or perhaps Mother becomes weary of the task and needs encouragement from Father. It is a fact that the sterner, more severe chastening given by a father will bring a child to rest and will reduce the need for a mother to become weary of the task.

"I delight to do thy will, O my God: yea, thy law is within my heart."

Psalms 40:8

8.

Identifying and Dealing With Rebellion and Self-will

Child discipline is only effective to the degree that parents identify and deal with their child's self-will and understand what constitutes rebellion. Is obeying a command halfway or eight-tenths of the way obedience or rebellion? When a child says, "Yes, Mother" or "Yes, Father" but does not do what you say or begins to do what you request but stops short of following through to the end, is this obedience or rebellion? Just when does obedience end and rebellion begin?

God's Definition of Rebellion

We have a classic definition of self-will and rebellion in the character and life of King Saul. In 1 Samuel 13:8 Saul was commanded to wait seven days in Gilgal for Samuel to come and offer a sacrifice. Saul became impatient and offered the sacrifice himself on the seventh day. Note verse 13: "And Samuel said to Saul, Thou hast done foolishly: *thou hast not kept the commandment of the LORD thy God,* which he commanded thee."

In 1 Samuel 15, the Lord commanded Saul to utterly destroy the Amalekites and all their possessions. Saul spared King Agag and the best of the sheep and oxen. In verse 13 Saul insisted to Samuel that he had performed the commandment of the Lord. Somehow, Saul concluded in his mind that partial obedience would be acceptable to God. It was not. Saul's excuse was that they had saved the best of the cattle in order to offer sacrifices to God. Verses 22 and 23 state a very important principle. "And Samuel said, Hath the LORD as great delight in burnt offerings and sacrifices, as in obeying the voice of the LORD? Behold, to obey is better than sacrifice, and to hearken than the fat of rams. For *rebellion* is as the sin of witchcraft, and *stubbornness* is as iniquity and idolatry. Because thou hast *rejected* the word of the LORD, he hath also rejected thee from being king."

God is saying that good deeds never atone for bad ones. To disobey under the pretense of doing something better is not acceptable. Saul thought that his way was better than God's way. God said it was rebellion and stubbornness.

What Can We Learn?

1. No act of disobedience can be justified. (We are not speaking about a command to sin.) Saul thought he had good reasons for disobeying God and Samuel. What do we as parents do when our children disobey and then excuse themselves and reason around their disobedience? It is a crucial question. Many parents give in at this point. It is easy to do. After all, from the child's perspective he had a reason for doing it this way. To consent to disobedience in his way is to fan the flame of self-will inherent in the child's nature and plant the seeds of humanism and situational ethics and ultimate rebellion.

2. Partial obedience is not obedience at all. It is outright disobedience. When you tell your child to pick up all the toys and he picks up eight-tenths of them and then runs off to play, is he obeying? According to the Biblical definition, the answer is no. Yet how often do parents look the other way and think, "Well, Johnny did pretty well." This kind of permissiveness on the part of parents is having a definite effect on the behavior patterns we see in many church situations.

The church makes rules or establishes standards of acceptable practice. Children who grow up in homes where partial obedience was acceptable find it very difficult to obey and stay within the established boundaries. They reason away the rules and excuse themselves rather then repenting and submitting. Who is to blame? Many times one can point to parental failure.

When to Begin

We addressed this point in a previous chapter. Yet it bears repeating. One of the earlier tests is establishing eating habits. The child is sitting in the highchair and decides that today he does not want to eat his vegetables. Father insists, but the child clamps his mouth shut and refuses to open. What do you do? The philosophy of the present day is to ignore the problem and hope that someday the child will learn to like vegetables.

This method is doing the child a tremendous disfavor. It is letting him have his own way and teaching him that rebellion is acceptable. It may seem innocent enough when the child is eighteen months or two years old, but when that child is eighteen and refuses to obey, who is to blame?

The Biblical way is to command the child to open his mouth and proceed to feed him. If he refuses he should be spanked. Repeated spankings may be necessary before submission is obtained. It can be a very painful experience for the parents and the child. The tender emotions of the mother and other siblings may complicate the situation. However, carrying the discipline through till the child submits is of utmost importance. In this process it is important that the one administering the instruction and the discipline stay calm but firm.

The follow-up after these early crises in teaching obedience is also crucial. After the child surrenders, take him in your arms and convey your love and acceptance. It may take more than one such confrontation. But be assured that if you are consistent you will be rewarded and your child will one day thank you for your consistent insistence on explicit obedience.

A word of caution in identifying this kind of rebellion. Be sure it is rebellion and not some other problem. Do not insist on large amounts of food. Be sure your child is feeling well. Forcing a child to eat when he may be ailing could be very counterproductive. Identifying rebellion requires a sensitivity to circumstances. On one occasion a young child insisted on crying in church. The parent took the child out of the audience several times and gave him a sound spanking. He only cried harder. Now, it was not normal for this child to respond in this manner. After the third repeat of this process, the parent discovered that a loose safety pin was hurting the child.

Discipline in the privacy of your own home. You may need to forgo discipline if you are away from home and you are in the beginning stages of teaching your child. Certainly this changes as the child gets older.

Listening to human reasoning instead of taking God's way is to forfeit the crown. King Saul tried to excuse his failure with human reasoning. It was either Samuel's fault or the people insisting on saving the best of the sheep and cattle. It is still happening. You tell your youth to be home by ten o'clock. They come home at ten-thirty. You give your daughter one-half hour to do the dishes. She fiddles around and takes an hour. It is Sunday afternoon. You tell the boys not to go down to the river. Their friends insist on going for a short time. They go for their friends' sake. Their reasons for disobeying sound logical, so we excuse them. But what are we teaching them? Are we not training them to be rebellious? When they learn that we do not mean what we say or that they can bend our word or justify their disobedience on the basis of what others are doing, we train them to travel the road to spiritual ruin.

If you are reading this and are convicted, what can you do? Repent! Confess to the Lord and your children your failure and chart a course that you intend to follow for the future. Our God is merciful. Certainly He will bless any honest effort to return to His way.

Young parents, refuse to be intimidated by today's looseness and parental laxity. It is not popular to bring your child's self-will into subjection with firm spankings. It is not popular to say no to your child and expect him to obey. Your peers may be saying, "Let them have their way; they will grow up someday." It may not be popular with men, but it is pleasing to God. Consistent chastening is an evidence of true love. Tolerance and laxness is in reality hatred. (See Proverbs 13:24.)

Consistent parenting is not always easy. There are times when your best effort may seem absolutely fruitless. God is trying to tell you something. "Without me ye can do nothing" (John 15:5). You need to humble yourself before the Lord and confess your faith in Him and in His way. Then pray for divine wisdom and guidance. Open yourself to others' counsel. Accept what others are observing about your strengths and weaknesses. Do not give up! "Weeping may endure for a night, but joy cometh in the morning."

"Iron sharpeneth iron; so a man sharpeneth the countenance of his friend."

Proverbs 27:17

9.

Coping With Peer Pressure

Henry emerged from his bedroom with a brightly striped shirt and tight Western trousers. Father, who was reading his Bible in the living room, glanced up with great surprise. "Why, Henry!" he exclaimed. "Where—and why—did you buy those sporty clothes?" "In town, of course," was Henry's quick reply. "My friend Amos wears this style. Why can't I?"

Ruth Ann peered into the mirror with glowing satisfaction. Or was it pride? She decided she would comb her hair like some of her friends did. By puffing up the front, moving the parting line, and dropping her hair a little lower over the ears, she produced the effect she admired in her friends.

Peer pressure! That powerful magnetic force that makes us want to belong, to be liked, to be included, to be in.

We often think and talk of peer pressure in the negative sense. The two examples above illustrate this fact. But peer pressure can be positive. When Christian parents bring children up "in the nurture and admonition of the Lord," those children will influence other children to go the right way. That is positive peer pressure. Let us note some objectives.

Parents need to be their children's best friends.

True friendship is built on love, trust, mutual interest, and sharing. It is expressed in togetherness, sacrifice, and in honest, open communication. It involves feeling and under-standing that penetrates into the depths of soul and spirit.

As children grow older, their circle of friends and peers becomes broader and more intense. While this is happening, their bent toward independence and distancing themselves from parental protection will no doubt express itself. We parents have three choices in this developing process.

1. We can take a nonchalant, irresponsi-ble attitude in which we simply let the child or adolescent find his own way, hit or miss. We do not involve ourselves with their ambi-tions or circle of friends. We just gradually go our separate ways. "Why not?" we say. "Let them have their fun. They have their own lives to live."

2. We can be overly protective. We can segregate our children from their peers. By keeping them in our presence and not allow-ing them to associate with others we can bet-ter control their responses. This method helps

the child to be an individualist. He is always right in his own cause, and everyone else is held suspect.

3. We can do it Jesus' way. His was the way of example, teaching, and reaching out to others. He was the influence (the right kind of peer pressure) that set the tone, established the priorities, and charted the course for others to follow.

We started by saying that parents should be their children's best friends. This requires closeness and daily communication. Encourage your children to talk about their interests, their projects, who their friends are, and what they are doing. Listen to their dreams, aspirations, and disappointments. Talk to them about your friends, your failures, and your values, and about how your heavenly Father (parent) is caring for you. Stay abreast with your children's thinking processes. How do they come to their conclusions? On what basis are they making their judgments? What trends are they following? Let them know you care. Let them know the high ideals you intend for them to pursue. Be understanding with their failures. Help them face disappointments with courage. Show them how to turn their mistakes and failures into steppingstones of progress. Your children deserve your confidence. Do not disappoint them.

Parents should be their children's best teachers.

We think of a teacher as one who presents a lesson and then proceeds to relate all the facts associated with how the lesson can be learned. Teaching is the impartation of knowledge. Our children, no doubt, will have many teachers as they travel the pathway of life. Some of these may excel us in their ability to impart knowledge. We can thank God for this. Yet in the teaching of moral values, principles of life and character, personal integrity, and responsibility, parents should feel primarily responsible.

Since we are speaking of peer pressure (the pressure that comes from other children), our objective as parents is to create a positive pressure that transcends any negative pressure. Every child desires to be well thought of by his equals. The dress code becomes a powerful factor in this respect. The two examples at the beginning of this chapter illustrate this fact. A three-year-old girl once came home from church and informed her mother that she wanted a pair of pretty shoes like her friends had. To keep in step, to appear alike (or better) to avoid being looked down on, is a normal response. We do not despise this fact. Rather, we want to steer it in the right direction.

It is one thing if a three-year-old wants a pair of pretty shoes like her friends; it is a much more serious matter when an eighteen-year-old insists on being in style like his friend. Somewhere there has probably been parental failure.

What are the basic principles and concepts that we begin to teach at an early age?

1. Right is always right, even if no one else does

it. Wrong is always wrong, even if everyone does it. Immediately some parents will object and say, "Who decides what is right and what is wrong?" What is right involves the moral principles of honesty, personal purity, modesty, respect, reverence, sobriety, kindness, forgiveness, gentleness, and any other virtue that expresses godliness. The three-year-old girl is taught that we do not buy shoes to look "pretty." Remember the adage "Pretty is as pretty does." It is not too soon to explain to a three-year-old about pride, covetousness, and envy.

It is in these early "innocent" stages of our children's lives that it is easiest to instill these concepts. However, it is important for parents to first learn them themselves. Too often we are inclined to consider it "cute" when children delight in personal vanity.

2. Others may be allowed to do things we cannot do. This is not done to instill a "better than thou" attitude. Rather, it is to help children realize their parents' priorities. How many nights in a week should youth congregate? At what age should youth receive their wages? How much free spending is permitted? How often are couples allowed to date? We could add more questions to this list. While we believe that the church should speak to these issues, yet we do allow some liberty of variation.

3. *Simplicity and contentment and stewardship.* We live in an affluent age. It is easy come and easy go. Young men can earn high wages if allowed to work in public. It is critical that youth are taught accountability in relation to handling money. The Scriptures are clear on the potential snare of money and riches.

For instance, Roger had worked in a furniture shop for a good wage. His parents permitted him to buy his own car at eighteen. He bought an expensive car on payments. Then he decided to buy himself a waterbed bedroom suite because it was the latest in sleeping comfort. He also saw an elaborate stereo set and decided it would be nice to have music in his own room. There were more and more things to buy. Roger complained that his paycheck just did not reach around.

Harry also worked at the same place. His parents taught him the principle of stewardship. He knew that his earnings were a gift of God. Harry felt accountable to give God twenty percent since he was single and had few obligations. At nineteen he was given permission to buy his own car. After looking at a number of possibilities with his father, Harry suggested that they wait a little longer while he prayed about the matter. He was not ready to spend all his savings on a car. A while later, he saw an ad in the paper for a repossessed car on which private bids would be accepted. It was just the kind and model Harry was looking for. He made a modest offer and was the highest bidder. The amount was less than one-third of his savings account. Eight years later, Harry was still driving that car, with over

200,000 miles on the odometer.

Today Roger is financially insolvent. But far worse is the fact that Roger is no longer a Christian. He is in the world having a fling, and is still unhappy and unfulfilled. Roger and Harry grew up together, went to school and church together, were baptized at the same time, and had worked together. Today they are an eternity apart. Harry was taught the principles of simplicity, contentment, and stewardship.

4. *The absoluteness of cross bearing and discipleship.* Adolescence is the time when most youth come to the crossroads of choosing their Master. Will it be Christ or the devil, the Gospel of salvation or the flesh and the world? Is it the narrow way of the cross or the broad road of self-pleasing and self-expression?

Jesus made it clear and plain: "Whosoever doth not bear his cross, and come after me, cannot be my disciple" (Luke 14:27). Somehow many parents manage to create a middle road. Certainly we make room for the immaturity of babes in Christ. But we dare not make room for carnality, casualness, and halfheartedness. Either you are with Christ or you are against Him; either you are gathering with Him or you are scattering abroad (Luke 11:23).

Crossbearing is the total surrender of the will. It enters into every phase of life. It affects who you choose as your friends, the way you comb your hair, the shoes you buy, the pattern of your attire, the places you go, the books you read, the tapes you buy, your work, your service, and your participation in worship. Youth who are taught the absoluteness of discipleship are not easily affected by negative peer pressure. Instead they lead the way in the path of Gospel truth and encourage others to follow.

Parents should be their children's best examples.

Would to God every parent could say with the apostle Paul, "Those things, which ye

103

have both learned, and received, and heard, and seen in me, do: and the God of peace shall be with you" (Philippians 4:9).

David said to Solomon, "*Know thou the God of thy father*, and serve him with a perfect heart and with a willing mind" (1 Chronicles 28:9). In spite of David's failures, he could still call his son to know his God. Can you? Would your children know what you are talking about if you admonish them on your deathbed to follow your God?

The historical account of Abraham and his son Isaac in Genesis 22 is very beautiful. "And Abraham took the wood of the burnt offering, and laid it upon Isaac his son; and he took the fire in his hand, and a knife; and *they went both of them together*" (verse 6). In the next verses, Isaac asked his father a pertinent question: "We have everything for an offering except for the sacrifice; where is the lamb for a burnt offering?" And Abraham's reply was, "My son, God will provide himself a lamb for a burnt offering: so *they went both of them together."*

Here is a son who had explicit trust in his father. Even though he did not understand the situation, he went with his father. In fact, they went together. That togetherness did not begin when they started on their journey to Mount Moriah. Isaac was no stranger to his father's devotion and worship patterns. No doubt he saw his father many times go to his flock of sheep and select the very best and offer it as a sacrifice to his God.

The very best that any parents can do for their children is to give them an example of sincere, humble, fervent devotion to Jesus Christ. This will be evidenced by a willingness to serve their fellow man in any capacity of need. Someone once said that "the greatest service we can render to our heavenly Father is to be kind to His other children." Every child needs that example.

Second to our devotion to Jesus Christ and the Gospel is Father and Mother's love and affection for each other. Isaac not only knew about his father's devotion to God; he was also well aware of his mother's faith and his parents' loyalty together in pursuing the will of God.

Parents united together in faith and love is one of the greatest factors in helping children cope with the pressures that come from their peers. Children know what their parents believe and why. They feel the security of their parents' love and trust.

In contrast children who see and hear their parents quarrel or hear them fret against divine providence or selfishly pursue their own agenda will be prime targets for negative peer pressure. This fact has been proven over and over. Dear parents, be today what you want your children to be tomorrow. With more faithful examples of parents becoming their children's best friends, best teachers, and best examples, there will be fewer Henrys, Amoses, Ruth Anns, and Rogers who fail to find fulfillment in the plain and simple path of life.

Parents hold the key to the direction of their children's travels. Do not make excuses. Do not blame others. Do not shirk your responsibility. *You* hold the key. And God will hold you responsible.

"And Eli perceived that the LORD had called the child. Therefore Eli said unto Samuel, Go, lie down: and it shall be, if he call thee, that thou shalt say, Speak, LORD; for thy servant heareth. So Samuel went and lay down in his place. And the LORD came, and stood, and called as at other times, Samuel, Samuel. Then Samuel answered, Speak; for thy servant heareth."

1 Samuel 3:8–10

10.

Character Development

The word *character* does not appear in the Bible. However, the words *integrity* (in the Old Testament) and *virtue* (in the New Testament) have the same basic meaning. "The integrity of the upright shall guide them: but the perverseness of transgressors shall destroy them" (Proverbs 11:3).

Integrity simply means an upright life, being the same all the way through, and the ability to control oneself in a time of crisis. Good character has been defined as the ability to recognize what is right, kind, decent, wise, and loving in every situation; having the desire to do these things; and acting consistently in accordance with this knowledge and desire.

Character in general includes all of a person's qualities or features; it is the prevailing nature of a person or thing. It involves moral strength or weakness. The special ways in which any person feels, thinks, or acts, whether they be good or bad, make up his character. Good character therefore is the expression of moral firmness and self-control.

Proper character development is important if we want to ensure a good foundation for congenial relationships in the home. Good character is an asset and provides a safeguard that helps the child cope with peer pressure. It is youth with sound character who come through the crisis experiences of life successfully. This is especially true when their lives are subjected to the control of the Holy Spirit.

Parents bear the primary responsibility for the development of proper character. Good character does not develop spontaneously. Children have to be taught what is right and then be required to do it consistently.

When we really get serious about building character into the lives of our children, we may need to go through a school of rehabilitation ourselves. Why? Because the deficiencies we see in our children probably reflect our own. Some parents are blind to their children's character deficiencies because they are blind to their own. Within a church body of faithful believers such a situation will be less likely to develop if parents are open to the counsel and observation of others.

Let us consider several specific character traits.

Attentiveness

Attentiveness is the trait of listening carefully to the one who is speaking. Being attentive causes a person to be alert to those from whom he can learn. It helps one to be sensitive to others who may be in need of help. Attentiveness is an absolute necessity for learning both obedience and safety.

Children who enter first grade and have not been trained to be attentive will be seriously handicapped. The child who does not listen to instructions cannot follow them. If he does not listen to the lesson as it is explained, he will not learn.

The Scriptures provide us with a vivid example of a child who was taught to listen explicitly. First Samuel 3:2–10 gives the account of God calling to Samuel in the dark hours of the night. Samuel responded immediately. Supposing that Eli the priest was calling, he quickly ran to Eli's room to see what Eli wanted. After the third repetition of this occurrence, Eli told Samuel to say, "Speak, LORD; for thy servant heareth." How many of our children would respond with such persistent obedience?

The child who has been trained to be sensitive to his parents and others when they speak to him will be better able to discern the call of the Holy Spirit when he comes to the age of spiritual accountability. Romans 10:17 says, "Faith cometh by hearing, and hearing by the word of God." The child who has not been taught to listen to the voice of authority will have a difficult time coming to the faith.

Hebrews 2:1 says that we should "give the more earnest heed to the things which we have heard, lest at any time we should let them slip." Revelation 2:7 says, "He that hath an ear, let him hear what the Spirit saith unto the churches." These and many other Scriptures speak to the necessity of paying close attention. Doing so just might make all the difference in our eternal destiny.

To develop good attentiveness, start early to speak directly to your infant. Call him by name and respond to his responses. As he grows require him to stop whatever he is doing when he is spoken to. Be satisfied with nothing less than an answer, at least a yes or

113

a no. A shrug of the shoulders should not be accepted as an answer. Test your child occasionally by having him repeat what you have said. Once a child is attentive, he is ready to learn to obey.

Obedience

True obedience entails doing what an authority figure asks us to do. It means doing it immediately, respectfully, joyfully, and completely. It is the opposite of doing our own thing.

Obedience requires the submission of the child's will to those who are in charge. The child must be taught this submission through the process of love and law. Because the child's will is set to do his own thing, he must be taught very early the meaning of the little word *no*. To learn this, he will of necessity experience pain and correction. Disobedience should always be understood to equal pain, suffering, and regret. Of course, the opposite will also be true: obedience brings happiness, approval, and satisfaction.

Obedience should have top priority in the parent's scale of values. No one can experience salvation apart from obedience. It is God who commands us to obey Him first of all. He also commands that we obey those to whom He has delegated authority, such as government officials, church leaders, and the boss on the job. Obedience is essential if the child is to attain to his highest usefulness in God's kingdom.

Obedience helps children to see love behind authority. As long as a child is allowed to challenge authority, he will see only what the authority is denying or requiring. Both he and the parents will be unhappy. Once the child is taught to submit his will promptly, he will be able to come to rest in his spirit and respect (that is, see the authority and wisdom of) discipline. He then will be able to enjoy the protection and security that come from being under authority.

To teach obedience effectively, the parents

should seriously consider their own obedience. Does the child see you bowing before the authority of heaven as you face your responsibilities? Does he see you going to the Word of God for direction? Do you consistently obey those who are called to shepherd the flock of God? Expecting wholehearted obedience from the child is futile if our own obedience is in question.

Teaching obedience requires that the parent be reasonable. He can require only what is within the child's understanding and ability to comprehend and perform. What is required must not go beyond safe boundary lines so that the child can come to realize that his parents have his best interests in mind. Consistency in this process, coupled with daily communication, will rivet indelible impressions and establish a mutual relationship between parent and child.

Contentment

Discontentment, which is inherent in the nature of children, means dissatisfaction with their present state and condition. It is an inner response to the things they see but have not obtained, such as another child's toys or possibly something they saw pictured in a catalog or displayed on a store shelf. It may also involve things that other children are allowed to do but that they themselves are forbidden to do.

Billions of dollars are spent each year on advertisements that promote discontentment. Newer, bigger, and supposedly better items are paraded before our eyes to make us dissatisfied with what we have. The covetous heart is appealed to in such a way that idolatry becomes a real threat.

Only the child who has learned contentment is happy. To accomplish this, the child's basic needs must be met. He must be nourished with a sufficient diet, he must have clothing appropriate to the climate, and he must be surrounded by love.

When these basic requirements have been met, parents should proceed by their example to demonstrate to the child that "things" do not bring happiness. The child must be taught that God is in absolute control of all things and that He has promised to provide for us all that is essential. The child must learn to feel gratitude each day for the little things of life and to enjoy them.

Children can be taught at an early age to amuse themselves by *creating* rather than by *getting*. Building structures from wooden blocks or putting simple puzzles together stimulates the mind more than the modern electronic toy that is nearly obsolete when the battery dies.

Contentment needs to be taught in relation to basic needs. It is important that the child learn to eat what he is served. He should not be allowed to decide his own menu. He must be taught which foods are essential for good health and then be required to eat them.

Children who are taught to be content with the necessities of life will be better able to cope with the temptation to become possessive and materialistic when they see their peers indulging in extravagance. Contentment will later help them to live a life of discipleship, which is nothing less than giving up all for the sake of Christ.

Neatness and Orderliness

The child is born into a confused and disorderly society. But God is not the author of confusion. He is a God of order. The whole universe functions according to His exact timing. It is sin that brings disorder.

Orderliness and neatness need to be taught and inspired. Children are not very old before they unconsciously develop concepts of order or disorder. Having a set bedtime and a regular time to get up in the morning is important. Encourage and insist that proper attention be given to personal grooming, such as washing face and hands, combing hair, and bathing regularly. Having scheduled mealtimes also enhances orderliness.

Orderliness and neatness have also been

defined as preparing oneself and one's surroundings to achieve the greatest efficiency. How true! Just think of how much time is saved when there is a place for everything and everything is put in its place. Small things like putting away toys, making beds, caring for clothing, and putting away shoes and boots are jobs that small children can do.

Jesus, when feeding the five thousand, left us a timeless example. He had everyone seated in orderly fashion. After everyone had eaten, what remained was carefully gathered up. Order contributes to economy.

Reverence and Respect

Reverence is a deep respect for God, for others, and for oneself. The little child should be taught very early to think of God with esteem because He is the highest authority. As the child's understanding continues to mature, this esteem should develop into a wonder mixed with love and fear. A proper reverence for God will also produce respect for those to whom God has delegated responsibility to teach knowledge and wisdom. Those authorities are you as his parents, the Sunday and day school teachers, the pastor, the employer, civil officers, and anyone else who is commissioned to maintain order.

Children who are not taught to respect others usually develop little regard for themselves or their peers. They will not care for their own appearance, dress, or speech. Besides manifesting unkindness and discourtesy for others, such children often fall into abuse of their own bodies and persons.

Lack of respect for others causes real problems for the teacher when the child starts school. It also affects discipline. Disrespect lies at the heart of many of the academic difficulties children experience. This is explained in the proverb "The fear of the LORD is the beginning of knowledge: but fools despise wisdom and instruction" (Proverbs 1:7).

Respect should be given to the property of other people as well as to their persons.

All property is owned by someone whom God has made. When children are allowed to abuse or destroy another's property, they to some extent destroy the owner's well-being and rob God by doing so.

By their attitudes and behavior, parents very early convey a sense of reverence or the lack of it. Parents who lose their tempers, raise their voices, or holler and scream at their children place those children at a tremendous disadvantage. Unless a sincere apology is made when this happens and an effort made to relate honorably, permanent damage will be done to the child's spirit. In contrast, parents who demonstrate appreciation for each other and for others—their in-laws, pastors, teachers, employers, and neighbors—plant seeds of proper respect in the child's frame of reference.

Parents should strictly forbid teasing, belittling people, jesting, and gossiping. The saying "If you can't speak well of a person, you should not speak at all" is worth practicing.

Conversely, the use of honorary titles, such as brother and sister, aunt and uncle, and sir and madam, will establish a sense of relationship that enhances appreciation for authority.

Forgiveness

Teaching your child about forgiveness is essential to sound character development. Forgiveness is the voluntary choice to pardon, excuse, and forget others' wrongs against us. It is the full, heartfelt release of any bitterness or resentment aroused against someone who trespassed against us. It requires relinquishing every desire to get even or to return the hurt.

Forgiveness also involves confession and restitution on the part of the individual who hurts and offends another. The child must learn not only to forgive others, but also to seek forgiveness by making confession, apology, and restitution when he wrongs them.

Unforgiving attitudes are the cause of many home relationship problems. Parents who fail to deal redemptively with their child's disobedience by correction and forgiveness immediately place a wall between themselves and their child. Guilt and negative attitudes that are not brought out into the open, cleared up, and forgiven will fester like hidden sores and will continue to erupt and worsen with time.

Children must be taught and shown by parental example that confessing wrong-doing is honorable and right. Every child should be privileged to hear his father and mother say, "I'm sorry." Children must also witness the peace that forgiveness brings when pardon is expressed and the matter forever closed and forgotten. To dig up the past or to rehearse offenses that have been properly cleared does a terrible injustice to any child.

The child who cannot feel forgiveness will not learn to forgive others either. Thus begins a course of life that will lead to many strained and broken relationships. Children run away from home, marriage partners divorce, youth turn to rock music and drugs, all in efforts

124

to escape the condemnation that comes from guilt that is not cleared and forgiven.

The Lord Jesus set the example for forgiveness. When hanging and suffering on the cruel cross, He looked down in pity upon His persecutors and said, "Father, forgive them; for they know not what they do." We who have received forgiveness from God will forfeit that forgiveness if from our hearts we do not forgive our brothers their trespasses (Matthew 18:35). Children need the assurance of their parents' forgiveness. They also need the example of parents who refuse to hold any accounts against another even if they have been hurt or offended by that person's thoughtlessness.

Honesty and Truthfulness

Without being truthful, a person will never be able to seek from God and others and to enjoy the forgiveness that depends on truthfully acknowledging the need to be forgiven. Without truthfulness a person is doomed to

125

having his word questioned and scrutinized—or simply ignored—even when he is telling the truth.

To escape the tragedy of living a life of deception later, a child must learn to be truthful from his early years onward. Truthfulness is a way of earning future trust by accurately reporting facts and events. A child needs to learn to gain the approval of others without misrepresenting the facts. For a child to be truthful, he must be taught to face the consequences of mistakes. Lying to avoid punishment will lead to other distortions of character and moral ruin.

The child must learn that truthfulness must start with *me*. Unless a child can be completely honest with himself, he will never be able to accept himself as he is. Without truthfulness he will never be able to seek help to strengthen the weak areas in his life, because he will not be able to face his needs honestly.

Being completely honest with oneself is a most difficult step. But it must be taken and followed by a determination to be totally and completely honest with God and others. Unless he is truthful, the child will grow up making excuses for himself, covering up, and exaggerating. He will isolate himself from others by a wall of falsehoods and distortions that he erects to hide behind. He will live with the constant fear that the lies he told to avoid the consequences of mistakes and failures will be exposed.

Teach the child early that "lying lips are abomination to the LORD: but they that deal truly are his delight" (Proverbs 12:22). Make your own life an example of truthfulness. Tell the truth when you are questioned about possible errors you may be guilty of, such as missing prayer meeting because something else seemed more important at the time. Be honest with your child and apologize when you misjudge or falsely accuse him.

Reduce punishments for offenses when the child tells the truth immediately after being caught in wrongdoing. Let your child know that an honest confession is always more honorable than lying in order to escape consequences. Praise truthfulness. Let your child know that it makes you happy when he tells the truth.

Above all, start early to teach what the Bible says about truthfulness and the evils of lying. Read stories about characters who were honest and refused to lie even when doing so seemed costly. Help your child to realize what the end of all liars will be (Revelation 21:7, 8), in contrast to the reward of those who are truthful.

Faith

Helping your child to develop a proper faith is another essential in building sound character. Faith in its simplest form is simply trusting someone to do what he has promised to do, or believing what is said on the basis of confidence without any other proof.

No child will develop a healthy character unless he has learned to trust his parents and believe what they tell him. The child's belief in God, in Creation, in history, and in his future teachers will depend largely on the degree of faith that he learns to have in his parents.

"Faith cometh by hearing" (Romans 10:17). The child who hears his parents repeat Scriptures or appeal to them for answers to the perplexities of life will develop a subconscious faith in this resource. Hearing you as a parent call upon God in prayer or praise and sensing that you love and obey the unseen God will furnish him with enough proof of the existence of the eternal God.

Faith is essential to the child's future salvation. Without faith it is impossible to please God (Hebrews 11:6). Therefore, it is of paramount importance that we as parents live by faith in relation to such issues as our health, our responsibility in the home and church, our financial obligations, and the normal stresses of life. A joyful trusting in God for daily strength and wisdom says much to the child about the indispensable element of faith.

Gratitude

Teaching your child to be grateful for all that he has and all that he receives is a virtue of lasting worth. The Scriptures give a vivid account of how unholiness always follows unthankfulness (Romans 1:21–32; 2 Timothy 3:1–7). Therefore, it matters much that the child be taught to say "thank you" and to sense appreciation for the many favors he receives daily from the hands of others.

Jesus' example of thanking God for the five loaves and two fishes and His calling attention to the one leper out of ten should help us appreciate the importance of gratitude.

When a parent expresses faith in the fact that God is all in all, that He is all-powerful, all-wise, all-good, all-loving, and is in control of everything, the child can rest in gratefulness that all his needs will be supplied. A child who feels grateful for his present circumstances will also know contentment and happiness.

Gratefulness also helps one to experience joy even in difficult times. Knowing that happiness and peace do not depend on congenial external circumstances but on a right understanding of God's providence helps the child to be grateful even in the face of adversity.

Being grateful will not only contribute to a contented life that is free from covetousness, but will also help the child to escape many sinful perversions. Rather than lustfully pursuing fleshly passions, the child can be taught the blessing of thanking God for his body and its functions and surrendering it all for His glory.

Cautiousness

The Bible warns of the danger of acting impulsively, of acting without thinking a situation through. "He that hasteth with his feet sinneth" (Proverbs 19:2). Without a sense of cautiousness, an individual can rush into a bad or dangerous situation. Cautiousness means being careful to do the right thing in the right time and in the right way.

Issues Related to Parenting

Carefulness is the quality of thoughtfully evaluating the possible consequences of decisions and actions before one acts. Cautiousness involves learning that unfamiliar situations may contain danger. It seeks advice and counsel before making decisions. It is the ability to see future consequences of present actions and decisions. Cautiousness also involves learning how to detect and avoid evil associations, as well as recognizing and fleeing temptation.

The child must be trained to be cautious. However, while helping the child develop a sense of caution, the parent must be careful not to generate unnecessary fears. A wolf is not lurking behind every tree, and certainly not every new, unseen circumstance poses a potential threat to the child's physical or moral well-being.

Developing cautiousness in a child starts with warnings concerning dangers in the house—the hot stove, hot water, sharp objects. The child who ignores these warnings will experience pain. Valuable lessons are learned by firsthand experience, but generally they are costly. Learning cautiousness in the home from both warning and experience will help the child avoid greater potential dangers outside the home.

Growing up, children will encounter a variety of temptations. The most dangerous are the sugar-coated ones—those that are accompanied by such challenges from the crowd as the following.

"How can you know if you don't try it?"
"A little bit never hurt anyone."
"We'll be careful to stop in time."
"Don't be a fraidy cat."
"No one will ever know."

Such arguments should send up red warning flags to the child or young person who has been trained to be cautious.

The blatant moral perversion of free love and sex is the result of throwing all caution to the wind. In the home the child must be taught to flee any person or temptation that

133

would encourage him to experiment with or gratify sensual impulse. Helping children develop the character trait of cautiousness in this area will help them avoid many other pitfalls and tragedies throughout life.

Patience

As well as training the child to be cautious, the parent also needs to teach patience. Patience is learning how to wait contentedly for the fulfillment of personal desires, wants, and goals. When a child learns patience, he also learns that God has a time for everything (Ecclesiastes 3:1–8). Such knowledge conditions him to understand in later years that it is for our personal benefit to wait upon God to fulfill His will in our lives.

Wanting something "right now" has led many people, especially the young, into many hurtful paths of sin. Entering into courtship prematurely and pursuing the urge to pet and caress have prompted many people to commit fornication and scar their lives.

Buying merchandise on credit has led many to financial bondage. Patience will teach us not only to learn to earn and save money before making purchases, but also to be willing to live without luxuries.

Patience is also reflected in good driving habits, for example, choosing to drive within the speed limit, observing and obeying road signs, and giving the other driver the benefit and advantage. Many accidents would be avoided if the Scripture "Let patience have her perfect work" (James 1:4) were followed.

Parents can help their children develop patience by not allowing them to eat between meals, by letting them reap the results of their own mistakes, by teaching them some skills, and by making them wait until they are sufficiently mature to date or drive. Children will also learn from the parents' own example. Seeing their parents sacrifice time and luxuries and wait upon God to meet their needs will act as an incentive to them to do the same. This is especially true when the parents demonstrate a happy, thankful, joyful, and contented spirit while trusting and waiting.

Security

Having looked at eleven basic traits of character, we will conclude with one more—a sense of security. To avoid fears, to achieve in school, to maintain a good digestive system, to sleep peacefully, and much more, children need to experience security.

True security ultimately stems from the knowledge that God is all-powerful, all-knowing, all-caring, and all-wise. It comes from the faith that believes that God will take care of us even when external circumstances seem to show otherwise. Naturally, the child is not born with this sense of security. Therefore, it becomes the parents' urgent responsibility to provide such a sheltered environment that will give the child this trust.

This trust and security will develop as

children see and sense that their parents have built their hope for the future on the promises of God rather than on material possessions, their own abilities, job security, pension plans, or personal savings, all of which can be taken away.

Security is also developed as parents provide proper shelter, food, and clothing. When a child has these essentials provided and is surrounded by love, he can feel secure even when normal situations and schedules are disrupted.

Affection and harmony between father and mother provide the child with a further basis for security. Then as he feels this love overshadowing him in spite of his worthiness or unworthiness, he also can become a stable factor in the lives of his peers.

As children grow older, parents should work to transfer the basis of the child's security from themselves to the Lord. This can only be done as parents help and lead their children to an experience of true repentance—

a repentance that confesses and believes that nothing of saving merit exists in one's own character; a repentance that embraces faith and confidence in the Lord of glory as the only one who can lead a person from where he is to where the Lord wants him to be.

In summary: The work of parenting is never finished. Character traits that were not discussed—such as meekness, diligence, punctuality, thriftiness, dependability, determination, flexibility, generosity, and loyalty—all add to the development of a child who can be of greater use in the kingdom of God.

Parental example in all the character traits mentioned is immeasurably important and valuable. Our children are largely what we as parents are. Their actions often mirror our own character. The more we express the divine nature and character of our Lord Jesus Christ, the greater will the advantage be to our children.

In this perilous and permissive age, let us

as parents rise up and shoulder the responsibility and the privilege that are ours, so that the generation that follows us may be able to say, "Thank You, Lord, for parents who loved me, cared for me, and brought me up in the nurture and admonition of the Lord."

Chapter 10, with some revision, is taken from *Growing Up God's Way* by John A. Stomer. Used by permission of Liberty Press.